I0605073

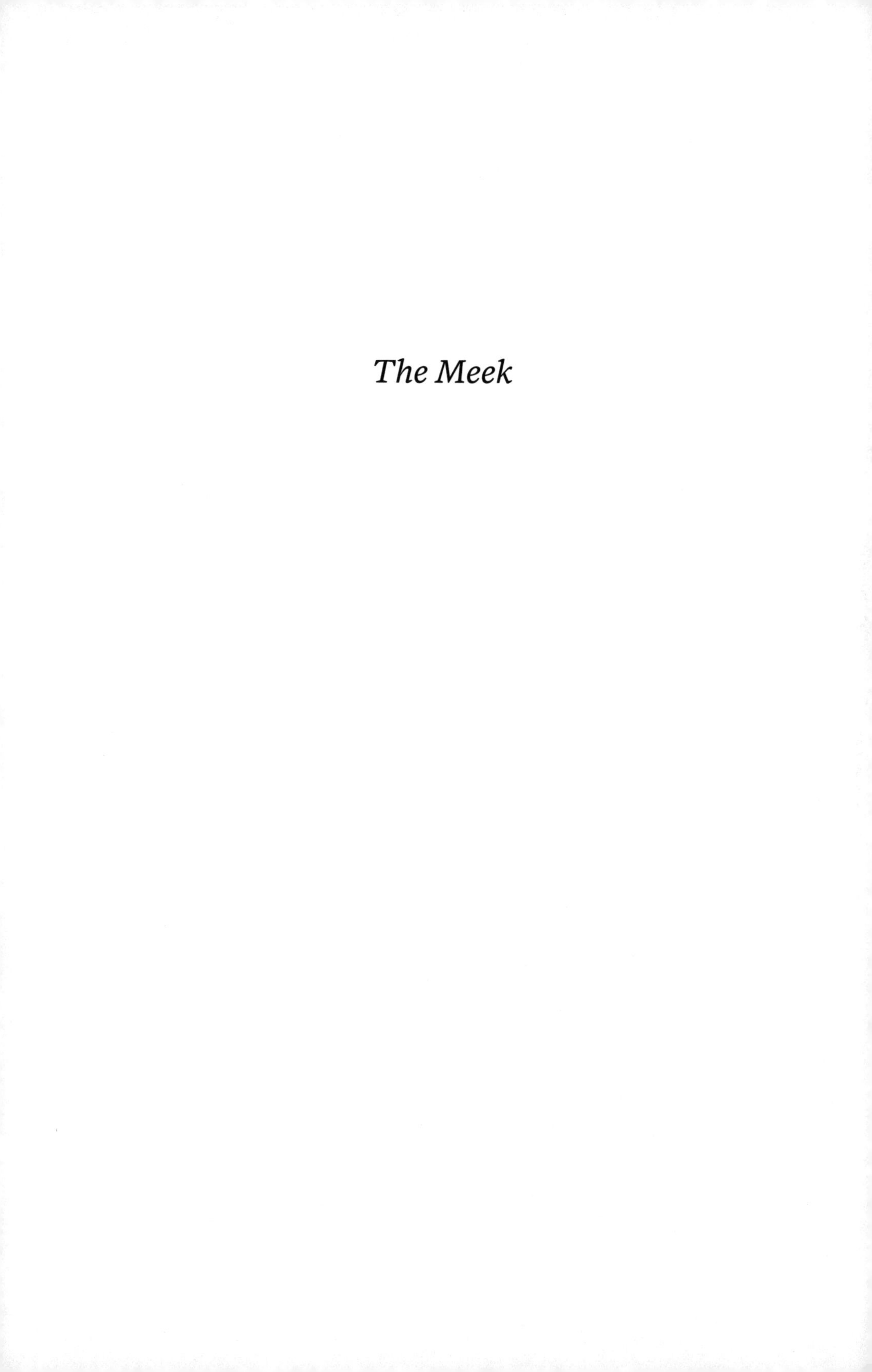

The Meek

the MEEK

Martin Dyar

WAKE FOREST UNIVERSITY PRESS

First edition

For permission, write to:
Wake Forest University Press
Post Office Box 7333
Winston-Salem, NC 27109
wfupress.wfu.edu
wfupress@wfu.edu

ISBN 978-1-943667-07-9 (paperback)
LCCN 2024930790

Designed and typeset by Peter Barnfather

Cover artwork: "MRI Diffusion, 2017" by Eilis O'Connell
(eilisoconnell.com), used with kind permission of the artist.

Publication of this book was generously
supported by the Boyle Family Fund.

for Rosie

CONTENTS

BUAINE NA GAOITHE

‘If we had a keen vision and feeling of all
ordinary human life, it would be like hearing
the grass grow and the squirrel’s heart beat,
and we should die of that roar which lies
on the other side of silence.’

George Eliot, *Middlemarch*

Burke's Goddess

On the phone, when the vet who was waylaid
sounded stunned by what Burke had just described,
and reasoned that the mare was getting worse,
Burke, although at first sorely grief-winded,
found within himself another cup of poise,
downed it quick, and then, as recommended,
brought the sweating goddess out of the yard,
and out behind the sheds to the meadow, where,
all her days, that always precious beast,
object now of true tenderness, had grazed.

She had, give or take, an hour of life left.
The vet would bless her warm, motionless bulk.
Which meant the final comforts she would know
would come from Burke: his loss-directed hands,
softly placed onto her pain-loosened neck;
and his unconventional words, through which he hoped
a light-headed, death-brimming horse might think
itself shielded by gratitude. He wished
that she understood him, and then sensed she did.
And so his palliative work went on.

Her lack of confidence notwithstanding,
when he told her to walk she acquiesced.
And then they lapped the field's October square,
transported, it almost seemed, into peace,
as they observed in tandem the old terrain.
Her two paths to the trough; the ghost Toyota
beyond the decommissioned iron gate;
the hawthorns, splendid on their plinths of dung.
And now, an aspect of the living hill
at the field's far end, a final juncture

of sightseeing in this time of despair:
she brightly gazes towards some half threat
(a figment, Burke believes, a nothingness
italicised, where a slope of young ferns
appears to rage beneath the wind's aura)
while he insists there are no grounds for fear.
He caresses her, and praises her, stopping
short of begging her to survive. And still
the labour of her courage-thickened lungs
communicates her end through his wet hands

and thereby makes him (as such things have before)
a soul unreasonable in the face of loss.
He stands back, looks at her, and then he reflects:
'She's past it, though alert. The signs are mixed.
The walking has imposed some pain relief,
but any moment now she'll try to kneel.'
And soon she does, pathetically and slow.
And Burke grows angry, thinking of his life
and life itself as heights of oblivion.
The mare gives him a weird, dependent look.

But, committed now to refusing love's
conscription, Burke makes no reply. He needs
his loss of hope fulfilled, and wants her gone.
And yet, in what is left of her, there's new
authority. What is it, there in the peat
of her eyes and in the weeping oaken mask
his heart refers to as a perfect face,
that tells him this platform of cold-blown grass
conceals a river which, all thoughts be damned,
they will bridge together for all time?

The Meek

She aimed the arrow of herself at welfare.
It was as if the animals had known how,
through some form of agricultural hoax,
some trick of animal telling, to cause
the truth of their deep suffering to coil
tight around her, and make of her their most
disciplined human agent, a woman fit
to put their world securely into words,
wear their mantle and be their steel-willed
outspoken saint of claws and hooves and meadows.
We, her followers, fear the price she paid.
Slaughter is the future. And yet we trust
in her cold acceptance of nature's cold view
that all of life is love misunderstood.

Two Surveyors

He knew two prisons well, he'd done bad things,
and sober nights, mostly, were out of bounds.
But I saw Loftus through his sister's eyes.

Last summer, when I met Maeve, she confessed
she doubted he would make it to Christmas.
And so I joined the group the guards had made

Loftus join, and picked rubbish through July,
a spy of the environmental kind.
Soon biodiversity had two new sons:

Loftus and I responsibly wandering
around the lake with lunches Maeve had packed.
Straight off he was obsessed with butterflies.

Otters too, but much more so butterflies.
He went like a bull into the whole subject,
catching dozens in fits of luck and guile.

I recall one. Off-white and silver-flecked,
with glossy blue seeds clustered at the base
of each antenna. In some way Loftus's

enthusiasm was an inner cross.
No, that's unfair. Mind you, the words I summoned
in the loss-resounding Loftus house tonight

were similar: that he knew joy, and found
he could talk his way through demonic days
whatever being hated made him feel.

On the Subtlety of Silver Birches

Just here, at the entrance to the carpark,
they cast around themselves a smoky veil.
It is subtle in its floating and its falling,
and in the ways it orchestrates the leaves.

It's subtler still in the work that it performs
for the sake of the unwitting passerby.
To phrase it medically, the silver birch
emanates a set of infectious gifts
geared more towards the soul than the body.

But, truth be told, there's never much of a yield.
A cold faith in nuance dogs these milk-bound boughs.
And mostly it's a springtime phenomenon,
one in ten thousand people made to think
the sun has aimed a birdsong at their chest.

A Lockdown Fox

As the fox became increasingly brazen
her daytime visits to the yards and gardens
that fell within the hill's crooked radius
caused more of a stir. It was a spring of plague,

and a time when nature seemed to be speaking
greenly through a hyperactive mouthpiece
of salvation and destruction at once;
if a young fox were to domesticate itself

in order to deliver the hill's signals,
and the better to inscribe love by circling
humankind in its fresh tower of fear,
it might be no great miracle. And yet
those paws brought ecstasy. The whole street felt
acknowledged by the earth, and longed for more.

The Plot

There was a plot to keep Anne in Dublin.
Five ex-boyfriends, myself the driving force,
met up for drinks and fed each other's need
to pin her down this time and make her see.

County Sligo, we'd heard, was in her mind.
And none would underestimate the draw.
Sligo, with those wide, butter-armoured dunes,
those copper-brained and summer-defying lakes,

where nature waives self meteorologically
and Donegal eagles mark Nordic time –
all this mirrored Anne's personality.
We drank her health and cursed her dream of peace.

But our sad friendships were subjective prey
to the drug of being Anne's man once again.
And so it came to nothing, except this:
she left us, Sligo won, she farms there now.

But today there's a primal photo in the *Times*.
A juvenile fox held in Anne's long arms.
I have read entrancedly, and now I weep
across the organic face of endless love.

The Shannon Reader

Here are her timetable vows: one hour
at the river, then two in the library,

and then back down to the river again.
This rhythm bore no automatic fruit,

but a day came when suddenly the whole
thing sweetened and deepened. She found herself

on first name terms with concentration's ghost,
while currents kissed the roots of every book.

She's upstairs now, the Shannon's own reader,
within whose work the otters can see themselves,

the one whose silence manifests a line
heard on the bridge, a line the sun makes true

by changing these black words into a shoal:
I read, I write, therefore all life is near.

A Launch Night for Cogitosus

In this parcel of miracles, completed
just this morning, and newborn now in your hand,
I have used the word *basilica* liberally.
But where I have I've meant *mound of nettles*.

And wherever the word *protectress* is used,
I wish to make (and hear me out) the image
of a mightily calm and nameless lake –
one that is brightly framed by February

greens and blacks – appear in the reader's mind
or (and bless them most of all) in the mind
of the listener. Brothers and sisters,
you will wonder as you digest my words.

You'll think Cogitosus the fluent ought
to be known as Cogitosus the dense
or Cogitosus the wilful waxer.
But hear me out. Straight language, from day one,

was simply out of reach. My true subject,
the woman in my head, was in my head
by virtue of being the woman in my blood.
Possession preceded imagination,

just as hallucination led to ink.
The woman in my head and in my blood
(the pole star, you might say, of all my rambling)
is a lakes-and-nettles character. And that's

not the half of it. Cogitosus the fluent
should have been, by being no reader, by
having a mind that was averse to letters,
a mind that seemed to despise concentration,

anonymous for all time. I was not
born for the fields of vellum. But she claimed me
as her own and, using for a shovel
a sunbeam, dug out of me my stores of doubt.

Brothers and sisters, she's a muscular
saint. I had been sitting early, beneath
the broad pink lava of a Curragh sunrise,
not quite at ease in my prayers, when she joined

the londubhery of the morning by
barking (yes, barking – show me a true healer
who has not employed dogs). And through my spirit,
'Cogitosus,' says she, 'you must unknot

your silence. My memory needs your labour.
Will you verbalise the land? Will you be my
anecdotal man?' How unready I'd have
seemed, brothers and sisters, had you seen me then,

wet-faced, hypnotised, while that Kildare sky
disgorged its tons of radiance and I saw,
beyond white walls that were and were not clouds,
a solar city inside a solar heart.

In the face of which, Cogitosus the fluent
barked, as a dog might when it tries to offer
a version of yes to its master. And yet
I had no master. She'd made of me a kind

of fox; for to be her narrator I'd need
to be both quick and strange. My vision ended
abruptly here. I watched her running off.
And the will to follow was the will to write.

The Green Hall

Because I once knew one of Paschal Convey's
daughters, I sometimes, despite the pitfalls,
permit myself to stop in the cold green hall
that leads back out from the toilets to the bar,
and there pay quick homage to his photo.

It's a great one. He was a saddler,
and one morning, twenty or thirty years
ago, some unwitting towny magicked
this immortal shot of Paschal Convey
in his workshop. There's the glow of a fire,

and the light of the sun through the window.
And the subject, sitting, his eyes shyly
beautiful, is cradling a new bridle.
Against my love for lovely Anna Convey
I'll sometimes call out 'Good man Paschal! Good

man Paschal!' as I re-enter the bar;
and yet what I am thinking is rarely good.
I'll find myself fending off Anna's words
after they've been freed from an old nuance,
or from a kernelled memory inside

a cracked-open impression of her father.
I gain a superstitious peace if I touch
the coarse wooden frame that houses that photo.
But it's lost if I don't swing laughter's sword
when my fellow drinkers read my burning mind.

The Cuckoo

'It's not like me,' he writes, 'to write like this.
But something, something potent, remains from
our cryptic exchange last week.' He feels,
and hopes she'll feel, in his infectiously
self-centred words, a tug of secrecy.

He complains that for her sake his fallen heart
ransacks his mouth for a tongue more fertile,
a mastery of rude yet emailable lines,
plain terms befitting a crisis of lust.

'I never write like this,' he writes, 'or dream
so primitively, as last night again
I dreamt of you. What is it, Kate, that weds
adultery to life and makes life ours?
We for whom an unspent kiss is death.'

Bread and Milk

What they found in Galway proved addictive.
It's strange to say that now, but no other
word quite holds the darkness they would reach
through those weekly Connemara retreats.

After the dabbling phase, there was scarcely
a Friday that they did not flee Dublin
direct from work, both of them helplessly
focussed on the bread of that seclusion,

and on the milk of how their souls behaved
in the wordless, oblivion-powered work
of their wholly indescribable sex games.
We judge them now, and lament them, because

it went so wrong. But, early on, we saw
only the blaze of eccentricities
that lit their single-minded journey west
and not their bid for God in nothingness.

Luck

They lost faith in their love, and called it a day.
That's almost fifteen years ago, much longer

than they expected to pine for each other.
They thought (they even discussed it) one focussed

summer of cold turkey would do the job.
A rough season crowned by a harvest of peace.

But they were wrong. The unremarkable seeds
of infatuation they talked themselves

out of have marked their lives. The truth grew wild
inside their separate hearts. It was, they've come

to see, a curiously tragic affair,
with its belated, drunk and circular

evidence of fullness. And its purity,
which in their strung-out prayers they call bad luck.

The Donnellys

Someone in an accent of seduction whispered *salmon*.
Then someone filled a bucket up with sleep.

Mermaidism in the Donnelly house
was five sisters deep.

A Television Gem

On the fifth day, in the mock studio
his wife Anne helped us create in the downstairs
bedroom, we interviewed Brennan's daughter.
Something in the way Helen entered the room
gave us pause. She'd kept us waiting, but a flint
in her grace insisted we put that aside.
She sat on an old dining chair we'd placed
before a dark and calm backdrop of oak
provided by a towering wardrobe.
And she looked at us – myself and my grinning
Dublin crew. We had become accustomed,
I suppose, to the biddable openness
and to the misty-eyed forthcomingness
of the lovely cast of characters that
visited the Brennan homeplace that week.
After what had seemed an endless lead-in,
an underfunded and amorphous thing
had come together wonderfully. A month
of ordinary editing turmoil
could lead us to a television gem.
Helen might have read on my face this thought:
'This bloody thing wants to direct itself.'
Or maybe the bedroom had begun to smell
of ambitiousness, which was separate,
of course, from the story of Brennan's
accident. Maybe, to Helen, our high
spirits resonated as a disregard
for her father, that tall absent-minded
presence who only now and then had appeared
at the window. An icon still, and, yes,
a living legend too, but primarily

now a gardener. And a gardener
in the most absolute sense of the term,
a fame-immune and damaged brain sustained
by the lifelines of flowers and vegetables.
Grant as they each did to the microphone
the warmth and wit of cherished memories,
not once that week had an interviewee
greeted or received a greeting from Brennan.
But Helen's arrival prompted a change.
Now he could be heard in the hallway. Once
or twice it seemed he was outside the door.
We all listened; though only Helen knew.
The sounds he made, his mumblings to his wife
for example (currents of dialogue
echoing suddenly in sorry rhythms
of distraction), were clan things that she seemed
ready to defend. It was as if Helen
had come to challenge our easy laughter.
Just as we were beginning to record,
her father, loud in the kitchen, said her name.
She made no reply and we overheard Anne
scold him softly. 'Have some respect,' she said.
'They're making this thing to help preserve your work.'
If we believed we were inscrutable,
Helen cut through that now. 'He used to be worse,'
she said, and we couldn't reach her with our
insistence that all week he'd been a sterling
host, a co-producer even. 'I have
no doubt,' I said, 'that he endorses the film.'
I added, 'Both your mother and father
have made us feel at home.' And the crew chimed in.

Helen chose and lit a second cigarette.
'This whole process is beyond him,' she said.
'The car crash brought two miracles: the blessing
of his survival, and the awful theft
of his personality. If you're telling me
you believe he knows you're here, then, either
you have not looked him in the eye, or you've
taken too many doses of my mother's
optimistic guff.' This was our rocky
start. A further deep silence was observed.
Helen's eyes were bright. Rain-spots were alive
in her long black hair. There was no escaping
the thought: 'For Christ's sake, she looks like her father.'
She took out her phone, and with her thumb dispatched
a long message, which had us all on edge.
But then she gave us a golden monologue.
Forty minutes of truth-filled fluency.
She invoked the dolmens of tradition
and imagination, caught Brennan's strange
gift, his work ethic, and his legacy,
as if in one breath of demonstrative care.
She ended with a mandolin commentary
that shone for being a touch didactic.
We leaned into our equipment and hid
our tension in the face of these jackpots.
To close, Helen swerved into a personal
account of how the accident had broken
her heart. At one point she mimed a two-inch
line on her chest, to indicate a crack,
the perpetual shock that had brought her 'two
decades of Dublin City lovelessness.'

‘The hell,’ she said, ‘of losing Dad, this way ...’
She gestured high, as if the walls held the guilt.
‘... Made it impossible for me to trust
that men were capable of sticking around.’
She seemed then to count out loves on her fingers.
What came next has ensured the film’s life.
The bedroom door opens and Brennan appears.
Helen doesn’t miss a beat. ‘I’m right,
she says. ‘You wouldn’t deny it, would you?’
‘Deny what?’ says Brennan, coming to her side,
his voice lowered so as to be in step
with all the mysterious protocols
that had possessed his home in that long week.
‘I’ve been telling them that you ruined my life.
The Tragedy of Helen Brennan should
be the title of this film, when it’s released.’
‘I ruined your life, did I?’ Brennan replies,
accepting a cigarette from his smiling
daughter. Next, Anne comes in, and we’re all cast
to the edge of the spell. ‘Left me in a heap,’
Helen says next. ‘Well,’ Brennan says, ‘No one would
guess by looking at you that you believed
you ever saw a man that caught your eye.’
As the camera captures all of Helen’s heart,
Anne gently dissuades him. And then he says,
as the cigarette gets confiscated:
‘Look at her lovely hair. If I ruined you,
Helen, the job I did was incomplete.’
‘Stop it,’ says Anne, ‘No teasing. Helen is here
to help.’ We laughed then, most of us, until
that unborn thing we’d trapped declared, ‘It’s done.’

The Neighbour

On the seventeenth floor
of the tower block, your
bravery evaporates.

Mary Higgins is not
a woman to be feared.
She is old and kind.

And yet the height and depth
of her isolation
repel your fourteen years.

She once clawed back her sheets,
revealing on her belly
a mass of bandages,

and asked you to touch them.
In a fire of shyness
you did, but nothing could

have steeled you against
the thick wound's pupation,
the fluent female pulse

of summers carried long
beneath a meat of pain;
nothing that day could make

consciousness safe. And yet,
a thing more unsettling still
is Mary's tendency

to monologue at length
about her mother's life,
her mother's athletic

gifts, her vague victory
against nineteen-fifties
Dublin. More unsettling

because when Mary talks
she really talks, and because
she rarely gets going

without arriving at
a ledge of wild-faced love.
Few fourteen-year-old boys
can excel in the art
of chauvinistic care,
but now you fantasise,

willing yourself a star
of flinty medicine.
You'd cull your emotions,

you'd bark a set of rules,
a set of strict timeframes,
you'd ban her darker talk.

But you won't now, will you?
You'll dawdle on the stairs.
You'll check the things you bought:

her milk, her cigarettes,
her sliced pan, her whiskey.
'God bless you,' she'll exclaim

repeatedly, being
possessed by gratitude.
And you will feel blessed,

despite the aftermath
of being brave, despite
being stopped in the hall

by a piercing welcome,
a guaranteed sorrow,
and ghosts that know your heart.

In Her Mother's Henry White Coat

> Henry White, the cream of the crop, when it comes to Donegal tweed. The colours reflect the Donegal seaside. This is gently worn, fully lined, no flaws. It has the label upside down. I would call that a glitch that doesn't affect the perfection.
>
> – Online seller's note, 2020

> Henry White clothing is unlikely to set the world of fashion design alight.
>
> – Lisa Godson, *The Times*, 2003

A timeless but heavy style, with a strangely
conceived fabric, a sense of moss and rust
lit from within by green woollen lanterns
and by the beaming quartzite signatures
of Donegal blues too confidently stitched.
A sense too of white clouds blossoming indoors,
white energy strapped to a badger's gusto,
a badger divinely groomed, a badger
whose black breast casts estuary light upon
a cardigan's wish to thicken and evolve.
Inside all this is her mother's politics,
her mother's heart broadcasting from the grave,
sending out drams of assertiveness and zeal.
Today is her mother's anniversary;
therefore memory works unjustly. Her mother's
knack of harnessing her daughter's conscience
has returned. Again she is led towards
enchantments based on a dream of divorce.
She goes to the door, turns, and swears back up
the stairs at the top of her lungs, so that

she might be heard in the courts of heaven
and across the listening Liberties,
and in the dark bedroom where he is lying,
feeling characteristically wounded,
as much by the blade edge his mind becomes
when faced with her grief as by understanding.
In the hallway mirror, looking and breathing,
she fixes the reflected world of herself.
These coat buttons are the eyes of self-respect.
These sleeves are living bandages that stop
the conflict in her wish to be embraced
as she makes a stab at freedom with these words:
'Tell me what my love means to you now.'

The View from Saint Catherine's Hospital

The strange wild-printed metal
of the bay is Catherine's face.
The queer grip of September
at low tide is Catherine's grace.

These fatalistic yellow leaves
perform a Catherine fall.
Touch this white-faced early sun
and you touch a Catherine ball.

These oystercatcher dramas
are bright with Catherine sound.
Scale this wall or leave this earth,
you'll land on Catherine's ground.

Pharmacy

in memory of Conor Walsh

Foxglove, I'm led to believe you can see my heart's
want of balance, even though, as a flower, your life
is a God-given blindness. They say too
that because of your poise, your personality,
you are alive to her need of a petalled voice,
one that will explain to her intimately
her own percussive heat, her doubt. Famously, thus
you've led bad hearts to the trough of wholeness.

If, Foxglove, you are true, then do not wait till
I have locked you in compounds to express
your deep vocation. Radiate now, this very moment,
speak out and boost my hands as I cut you
here in this steep, wild, vapouring,
blue-roofed County Mayo drain.
And listen carefully, and more than carefully, with me,
as I listen to the bright declining bird my wet shirt shields.

Like a Soul

in memory of Mícheál Ó Súilleabháin

We'll speak now, for a brief moment, although,
you understand, I would prefer not to
have to press you again on the question
of your self-confidence. You're supposed to be
past all of that. Remember what I said
on the first day. I have a role. *Professor*
fits by sleight of hand only, but we must
for practical purposes use that word. We'll
also use *mentor*, another wiry title,
which you must think of as equivalent
to your solid demon of encouragement.
I am here for you. And yet, the nameless
pilot in your heart is the primary
authority in all of this. Make no
mistake, that little man knows our business.
After today, I won't repeat myself.
Today we cross the Rubicon of music.
But I'll spell it out for you now, one more time:
you were born for magic, and born for this.
Pack all of your faith into that queer notion.
You were born for, and born of, magic. Of course,
we'll be keeping this to ourselves. There are some
who at the faintest scent of our ideals
will begin to orchestrate our downfall.
The sweet juice of hatred is plentiful
hereabouts. But that is for down the line.
This morning, let your writing be a war
for the territory of concentration.
Go back to the irrational daydream

that the songs you are trying to attain
are a means to part the veil of the West.
Stay with the coastal hills. Marry their slopes,
marry their streams. What was your Pied Piper
image? Something about imagination
being a cave in Limerick? Don't dare let go
of that romantic fragment. In fact, repeat
it to me for the remainder of the year.
Give it to me a hundred different ways.
Relentlessness deserves to be in the room.
Sit at the piano now, and begin
with a pair of chords. Play them, mind you, gently.
Let's aim to reach the most original
gentleness by midday. Pied Piper stuff.
Subtle, careful, merry, plain, and true;
a tune that makes the heart look like a soul.

John Reilly's Audition, Roscommon 1966

On entering that near-eclipsed pub in Boyle,
the collector received a proud nod from Dodd,
the owner of the place, who the night before
had promised: 'I know a Traveller, a man
so full of old songs it would frighten you.'

Dodd's eye cast a curatorial light now
towards an isolated drinker by the fire,
a dignified clown: ruined boots and teeth,
generous eyes, unreckonable age.
'When I say full,' Dodd had said, 'I mean full

to the brim.' He had overblown it, more than
likely. Or had he? The required ghosts were
in John's speaking voice, round a tree of verses
that swivelled when he sang and caught all hearts.

Glossopdale Folk Club Forever

> *All the songs on this record have been learned from books, tapes, records and scraps of paper, all sent to me by friends that I have made around the folk club scene. I hope that the songs haven't been damaged too much in transit.* – from the liner notes of the Nic Jones album *Penguin Eggs*, Topic Records, 1980

On the road home, sometime after 2am,
the pit of 1982 got darker.
In the echoing lane behind the club

his beaming audience, made up it seemed
of little more than three local families,
had waved him off. Another transcendent gig.

He then drove twice across Glossop Brook Bridge,
accidentally circling back to the venue
where future nights were sealed again in laughter.

And then off he went alone down winter's road.
He should not have survived the crash. This is
a key to the legend. Death had won outright.

But death's bold owl rose inconclusively
from the flame-littered meadow. Similarly,
his long years of healing have had no logic,

beyond, perhaps, deep guitar addiction,
the cooperating hearts of grateful songs,
life's thirst for life, and the Glossopdale effect.

Earth Radio

It's five years since the Goat O'Hara died.
Tonight he was publicly remembered
in a manner that some in the town would say
showcased the O'Hara's oddness once again:
an hour of stargazing on Tumgesh bog.
The Goat was struck by a car not far from there.
It was a drunk-driven car, and he himself
was drunk, heading home long after closing,
a laneway shade, waddling and unaware.

For his two brothers the loss was immense.
They'd been a trio of farming bachelors,
and the pair were ill-equipped to handle life
without that threefold tangibility.
So Frank and Luke forced the door of the past.
The Goat had long claimed he'd been taken
by extra-terrestrials: twice in his teens,
again on the night after his mother died,
and again on the night of his fortieth.

When cajoled to tell the story in the pub,
he could always flummox a new sceptic
with his conviction. Slivers of truth,
glimpsed both in his way of recounting
the mood of interstellar politics
he said he'd sensed in the queer medicine
of his captivity, and the grey footnote
of his abduction dates, gave him an air.
You'd mark him a local man getting drunk

in capitulation to heavy wonders,
a good man flanked by two similar types,
drunk too, but estimably listening.
It seemed that half the town was there tonight.
'Hard to believe it's five years, God help us,'
we said, as Luke and Frank shuttled us out,
five nervous loads in two battered tractors,
fording as no car could the sunken tracks
that lead abysmally to the chosen field.

The floodlit scene was not entirely mad
for those who'd been involved in previous years,
but the smiles of newcomers told you their minds
were blown to the greenest incredulity
as Frank and Luke with microphones denounced
the night sky for its cold conspiracies,
spoke echoingly of transcendental ships
undoing every farmstead in their wake,
and then, for sibling drama, killed the lights.

Flannery

Flannery was not a well-regarded vet.
Horse people tended to see straightaway
the fear his joking eyes sought to conceal.
Hating the roar of his jeep, cattlemen
spoke with flamboyant harshness when it passed.
Some swore his urban airs would bring a death.

Yet Flannery's business lasted five years,
the sore, elemental need of a vet
preventing us from venting face-to-face
the widely-held opinion that he was,
at best, a dogs and cats man who made farm
calls only out of vanity or greed.

Two brothers who'd spent countless hours online
researching ways of being vets themselves
(or close enough) met the locum in town.
And soon the story found a hundred lanes.
Flannery became an emblem of distress.
Authoritative slander was now hushed

in favour of fraternal commentaries
on what depression meant; and on what women
could do to men's spirits by calling time
on a half love, or, worse, on a true love,
which overnight had ceased to anchor them.
Three counties wondered darkly in tandem.

A number said he'd butchered his own arm.
Most doubted this while echoing reports
of bandages and guards and hospital.
The girl he'd lost was readily recalled:
a wealthy type, a student who had come west
on consecutive summers. With her wit

she'd left the gates of sentiment open
in many a yard when August bore her off.
Tonight, pub-mumbled empathies persist.
Words along the lines of, 'Flannery neglects
himself. All vets, good and bad, are the same.
Most of them, mileage-mad, live without sleep.'

And, 'Look, if livestock is not your calling,
and you're drinking (I heard he drinks alone),
if you're in workaholic territory,
and then a girl comes, a flower maybe,
a joker, and a better vet – Well, look,
you're not a man at all if you stay strong.'

Odd One Out

I have fallen into the habit of stopping
at an old gate, on a path that leads back
to a lane that leads back to a quiet road;
and seeking conversation with a group
of shaggy ponies. The sun is almost out,
I have just finished my remote routine,
my fledging dialogue with the Irish Sea,
my cold equilibrium appointment,
and now I march myself towards the town.
Remembering the pony field, I'll turn
and go through bushes, down a slope, to where
they tend to be, assembled closely round
the pathetic bounty of a silage bale.
Lesser farmers give to lesser horses
a surplus share of lesser cattle food,
a thought that sends my eye further into
their long field. There is no grass to speak of,
a topic comprehensively set down
in a script of muck and stone. There's a bank
of rubbish down the left side, near a cliff.
A pair of banished ovens and three rotting
bikes are a scene of headless nativity.
And a toppled cairn of tractor parts confirms
a no man's land unthinkingly sustained,
a petty hell the fencing's overdone
marriage of tattered ropes and barbed wire
makes more true. Near the dead centre of the field
a white water tank is resting on its side.

For all the world it looks as if, almost there
but reluctant to be shown the sea,
it threw itself in protest from a trailer.
For more than a month, after a cursory
set of glances, the ponies duly paid
no mind when I appeared. Address
them as I might, their trodden feast could not
be trumped by the noise of a hooded man.
But this has changed. Three times now my visit
has entailed a new routine. A glorious
odd one out has joined our early family.
Some kind of hawk (maybe a kite) has taken
to perching on the tank – only a short
stone's throw from the fodder, but faced away,
its pleated copper shoulders turned against
the gate, its full size neatly suggested
by the snugly withheld scabbards of its wings.
I take two steps. I've been seen, but the bird
goes very still. What is discernible
as movement before what follows (a show
of flight, a singular dark wing beat
that happens in the span of my third step
and sends the water guardian into
the next farm) suggests a fabulous grade
of violent-minded shyness. It is gone,
but I have been inside that raptor's wits.
And I have felt the field's claim on the world.

So much so that to turn to the ponies
is to sense a dream undone, as they, glossed now
by the flow of the sunrise, make their own
adjustments. These past three mornings, breaking
the breakfast circle, the least of them has come
to the gate. The politics of horse life has
given that lean creature a task. He won't
let me touch him, but he lingers and he looks,
and he says two things in wintry confidence.
'The food is not for sharing' is the first.
And he adds, to this necessary statement,
a piece of January guff, which doubles
as a blessing, a trespasser blessing.
Four fenced-in syllables: 'You frightened her.'

The Poster

It is beautiful and memorable and yet
at the same time it is over the top.
The poor health of tourism is on their minds.
That is why the artist has built this story
of pure and irrepressible welcomes.
Athlone Town looks like a patchwork volcano
across the terraced face of which local things
insist that local life is heaven's gate.
Everywhere there are incidental dreams.
Cormorants are fearlessly queuing up
outside this café. Here, in a carpark
beside a funeral home, a game of cards
holds three costumed elderly men spellbound.
These four sycamores have cathedral status.
The mouth of this dark alley somehow says,
'Immortal views, my friend, are rooted here.'
These bright windows look down on this parade
of strangers armed with far-fetched gifts. Down here
the River Shannon is a voluptuous
avenue that brings the beholder's eye
up from a dark foreground to the patterns
of this bridge, on the solid grey span of which
the near forgotten Athlone novelist
and baker John Broderick stands, a hero
recruited posthumously to shore up
the town's self-confidence. In his left hand
he clutches a giant quill (greater than
any imaginable donor bird)
and in his right a mighty loaf of bread,

not unlike a bulging schoolbag. Broderick
is smiling, his face angled at the peace
of a lemon-cheeked sun affixed above
the glow of the river. To look at this
Broderick cartoon, with its blue three-piece suit,
impeccably water-lit and boy-faced,
is to receive from the artist a dose
of neat charisma. But not everyone
is persuaded. This morning, when the poster
was publically unveiled outside the civic
offices to a group of council staff,
a woman in her nineties from the town,
who'd known the Broderick family well,
stopped for a moment on her daily walk
and declared that the likeness was not right.
A twenty-something politician, with
a debutante's effort of control, asked
was it the fact that Broderick was smiling?
(He had wondered if bookishness could be
separated from broodiness and still be
an instrument of prestige.) To which
the woman replied, 'It's not so much the smile.
Broderick, in his grave, would be turning for joy
at this belated bit of prominence.
Certainly, he loved Athlone, and would be
one-hundred-per-cent behind your poster.
It makes sense to me that you have him grinning.'
Her quibble, rather, was biographic
and personal at once. 'You must remember,

being from a town means you see people
in a given light. That light can mislead,
it can be unfair; it can be corrupted
by stories. But it can also hold pure truth,
by virtue of the way a person's life
gives off a light of its own. Broderick
loved his mother. They had more than mothers
and sons ordinarily have between them.
They were fast friends and their world was humorous.'
The council group were tense now, but they listened.
'For my eye, if there's one Broderick on that bridge,
there's two. Mother and son, crossing as one.
But, to my knowledge, after his mother's death,
poor John could never bring himself to make
that simple journey again on his own.'
A tall man who felt he had the woman's
measure now, butted in for the poster's sake:
'Maybe he is smiling because he's thinking
of his mother.' 'Yes, that would make some sense,'
the woman replied, 'and the bread in the hand
would chime in that respect too. His mother was
wedded to the bakery. The quill, though,
would not be right, if we're talking about
smiling in communion with his mother.'
The young politician asked, 'And why is this?'
The old woman's tone held fresh conviction here.
'Because the writing represented trouble.
They'd blocked it out. She would never ask John
about his books. She knew too well the pain

his efforts brought. Every day she gave him
in that regard a gift of silence meant
to keep him going.' 'Surely,' someone said,
with added chauvinism, 'surely she
read the bloody books.' Here the old woman
stepped backward, a moonwalk. 'I'll go,' she said,
'my doctor has me sworn to do a mile.'
She fielded their chorus of kind wishes
and then, calm in her rivalry, she said:
'They had a pact. The books did not exist.'

The History of Medicine

for Bernard

Traveller, rest here a short while. In this village a doctor
once befriended and healed an injured wolf.
For one summer they were companions.
        No, they were collaborators.
Many from this place, now dead and gone,
        saw it with their own eyes.
A small but wholly convincing group was gathered
the night the wolf presented its healer-master
        with a cow that was in calf.
In the end, despite taking himself off to Dublin, the doctor
failed to set down the scientific substance of his story.
Neither has the deep linking of his spirit with the wolf's ability
to illuminate the history of medicine been communicated.
Something falls to me perhaps, an old man,
        with this knife in my hand.

I who as a boy saw the doctor and the wolf swimming
together, up in the smaller of the two lakes, and thought
to myself: how like brother and sister, and how thin they both are.
The cow was grazing nearby,
        and I noticed they both looked to her
every now and then in vigilance. The bullrushes whispered,
'The wolf's brain is the thing he has healed, and not its paw,
or not only its paw.' I carve these words here
        in good faith, and as it were
with a double spice of mature hearsay and mature village pride.
And I send them forward thus for the likes of you,
who, being on a journey, might have the best heart
for an abbreviated and honest fairy tale.

The Cliff Flowers

translated from the Irish of Liam O'Flaherty

I said to the flowers,
'Yours is a joyless, a crappy home,
not much more than a cliffside prison.

Nothing below you but green stone
and the filth of the birds.
A foggy and almost illicit place,

a place of coughed-up brine,
to which, from one end of the week
to the next, the sun makes no gladdening visits.'

But the flowers cordially replied:
'These facts to us are nothing.
We are spellbound by the music of the sea.'

The Mapping of Limbo

Down here there is no sun,
no image of the day to speak of.
You must be forceful
in your concentration.
Cold cartography must
define your heart.
Because the children will come.
They will swim around you,
hungry for play.
And you must disdain them.
Against the great dream
that is the light of their need,
it falls to you, worker,
to be a counter-dream.

Hansel and Gretel

I recall it this way, sister. We had escaped
through the attic and climbed out onto the roof
of the cottage. Hoisting each other then,
we stood astounded on the sun's highway.
And then, embracing grievously, we leapt,
or maybe we dropped, down to that garden where,
although vitality was beyond us,
our sibling mettle quickly re-emerged.
Twice we shot around the dark boundary,
a pair of volatile waifs, voicelessly
begging sycamores to direct us home.
But before the way could reveal itself
the witch appeared. I recall that I sprinted
angrily, recognising how those vain eyes
and that lie of nonchalance sought to claim
that she was much more than hatred's magistrate.
And the madness of my running made you fall.
But if it did, soon you were left much worse.
You don't remember this. The stones she threw
travelled slow. She'd sent them not what you'd call
accurately, or even with purpose,
but, it seemed, in defeated rehearsal.
Characteristically, she abandoned them,
her sentient projectiles, on the air,
and then went black-mindedly back indoors.
You'd think she couldn't bear her own powers.
But she was, of course, part witch and part actor,
the latter uppermost when, like that, making
much of disdaining violence, she told those
recruited stones to rain down on our lives.
Your dying commenced quickly. You became

an image of yourself, a brow of dusk
inside a luminous mask. But while I saw
and felt your story slackening, and though
I knew, seized as I was by full instinct,
that I must say goodbye, that I must be
in the face of death more than a brother,
still I spoke in denial. What did I say
to bring you back, you ask? Maybe I said
babblingly, 'Have courage.' Or maybe,
'Sister, since you are more than half my heart,
it's wrong of you to heed a second fate.'
Whether such thoughts held sufficient spark,
and whether, through my cursing, some great hand
stirred and knew to transfer the unnatural
fund of pain that had replaced my tongue
into the purse of the woods, cannot be known.
But sister, let's go on, and let's pretend
that what we've lost was dreamt, and that the sun
will shield us both against the glare of life.

A Tower

Rapunzel, let down your hair to me.
Alone I cannot climb
the swells of thorn and masonry
that draw the blood of rhyme.

If I Am Caílte

They'd had six months of brilliant talk and touring,
and Patrick, though not known for his patience,
had listened at length, hosted tactfully,
and indulged the presence of this wizened
little man, this pilgrim, for whom body
and time and death appeared to have been released
like fish, for Ireland's sake. He had come out
of the deep past and his name was famous.
A hope-inducing, many-sided name,
a name that was an energy: Caílte.

Six months. And they had made good use of him.
When Patrick gave the documentary signal,
writing teams formed fastidious circles
around Caílte. Translators; memorisers;
eager ink boys; elite lyrics women;
fiction heads who loved to spool the real
and whose talent was the fear of forgetting;
coy listeners too; shrewd intuitives; great
arresters of the mortal ways of words.
And, by Christ, did their weird guest give them work.

Point to any mound, any rock, or ditch.
Point at a well, a tree. Query a river's
or a lake's character. Choose a name within
a name. And ask Caílte about its roots.
He was a channeler of enigmas. 'It's
easily told,' he'd say; and then off he'd go,
his heart an etymological spring
that loved to offer up, from caves of lore,
supernatural takes on local things.
He told them what could not be told, and nursed

their senses with the saga of the earth.
All of which was gold for the missionaries,
who, despite their own abundant talents
and despite their kitty of miracles,
had dreams of dominance that wanted style.
As Caílte toured the provinces, the force
of his imagination made the face
of the new religion brighter and more true.
His voice a kind of holy advertisement,
from mucky platforms in Roscommon, Limerick,

Kildare, Armagh and Mayo, fine onslaughts
of Roman credibility were launched.
Small wonder that they cajoled and pushed him,
and so relentlessly. But a day came
at the end of that marathon season
when Caílte began to show signs of strain.
Patrick was quick to dismiss the members
of his retinue who felt compassion
and concern at the little man's shrillness
and paleness, and those who thought it an omen

that he seemed so unmoved by his own powers
(a demonic humility was mooted).
Several sought Caílte's ear and begged him not
to risk upsetting Patrick. 'Give us one
more month,' an anxious boy beseeched. 'Be strong.'
But to no avail. Caílte had succumbed
to what one cleric deemed the residues
of his own youth, days long lost but now exhumed
through recollection on the grandest scale:
'His gifts of memory all come from disease,

and that disease is now his mind's terrain.'
Caílte was not for marshalling. 'My heart
is breaking,' he said, 'and I'll tell you why.'
They were camped remotely and high; below them
three counties ranged away from where long swathes
of heather united two narrow glens
and a forked half mile of forest caught the sun.
Patrick tried to speak, but Caílte, self-consumed,
cut him off, which caused a chain of uneasy
smiles to circulate at Patrick's expense.

'I remember too vividly,' Caílte said,
'the company of my friends. My heart is tricked.
Where are they all, it asks, in an innocence
that I treat watchfully. And yet today
I too am tricked. Like a cracked heart I look
about me, waiting for the morning's doors
to admit men long turned to dust, men long
used to being dust.' 'You came to us, Caílte,'
said Patrick, urging order with his tone,
'on a mission that has become dovetailed

with our own. You came, may I say, as a prize
from the Lord.' 'No,' Caílte replied, 'no,
I came in order to become myself,
to become fearless Caílte once again.
I intended to hunt and fight, but instead
I have worked in names and memories.' Patrick
cut in: 'Yes, you are our quarryman of words,
and we have worked with you, we have preserved
what you found ...' 'If I am myself,' Caílte said,
'I should do more than that.' Patrick insisted,

'Your mission has entailed these divine feats
of memory.' 'But if I am Caílte ...' There
was a silence. Caílte went to his knees.
Sternly Patrick instructed all present
to stand and prepare for an onward journey.
It was suggested they might carry him.
'No,' said Patrick, 'We will leave him here.'
Preparations began. 'If I am Caílte,'
the kneeling man cried, 'I should have a means
to cut the cords of grief inside my chest,

and I should not be beholden to this crowd.'
'Caílte,' Patrick barked, 'you are dying.
You are Mary's own carrion now.'
A woman raised a swift hand in caution.
Caílte's body was changing. They watched him.
He seemed to be taking the form of a bear.
Disgusted, Patrick turned away, then said,
'Thank you for your service. I release you.
We shall honour your stories.' 'What stories?'
the suffering bear replied, 'I have not begun.'

Revelation

When the time comes, and when, once again,
        it has been decided
that I am the appropriate oracle,
        and if you happen to be the one they send,
you will find me in the townland of Kilbride.
        Come confidently into
that quiet domain, allowing yourself
        to be possessed as fully as possible

by the words that have been entrusted to you.
        If I might instruct you
further, let me add: when you see me,
        do not yield to fear at my appearance.
Depending on the day, I might be in one
        of the lower fields, a boggy place,
and, in all likelihood, you'll find me greatly changed.
        Not a recognisable

sort of man, though I remain always a human figure.
        I might be expanded,
even to the size of an elephant.
        But I beg you, do not be intimidated.
The essential truth is not frightening.
        I am merely absorbed in my work.
This must be understood,
        otherwise you will become disturbed.

Last year, a messenger spoke of me as follows:
'On the side of his neck
there was an almighty wound,
two feet wide and more, which seemed to serve
as a second mouth. He seemed to be in pain,
seemed angry from pain,
but at the same time, out of this wound,
he was giving birth to owls:

dozens of them came out of him
while I was standing at the gate.
There was beauty in it. Cautious white forms
appearing and flying off.
Some seemed, in high rain-bolstered circles,
to be guarding their birthplace.
There was also a hive sound, a purposeful humming,
which became fraught

each time an owl took flight;
and then the wound would flex and right itself.'
Previously sober for an unprecedented run of months,
this local man,
because of an unfamiliar weight of wonder,
went permanently
back to his drinking. But you now have
a set of shielding images. Remember,

I might appear grotesque (bull-like or rhinoceros-like)
        and I might be lost
in the apparently divine act of expelling
        new-fledged birds from a chamber
inside my throat. Will you do what you have
        undertaken to do? Will you
communicate with me? Will you come
        into the centre of the field?

And will you bear your message fully?
        Will you bear it to me, even if,
instead of being hideous, I prove invisible?
        You seem resolute. Well,
let us promise then, for the sake of the question
        of extinction, to be a pair
of unyieldingly loyal comrades. Bite down,
        messenger, on that old word, *oracle*.

Come to the outskirts of the town,
        cross the outer road, and cross the river,
and carry, like a strength enthroned within yourself,
        this plea: *Let the coming*
extinction be revealed. Let the coming extinction be revealed.
        You'll find me,
I trust, with neither difficulty nor fear,
        in a field in the townland of Kilbride.

The Children of Lir

Look, look, there they go.
They're flying from my verse.
A sentence made of centuries –
there's no more perfect curse.

At the Court of the Curlews, Magheramore

Why trust the extended beauty of this lane?
Why trust these trees? Old oak power and old
pine character, and this blend of holly truth,
mixed in with holly's oil of memory.
A remote winter lane which by virtue
of the sea's closeness seems to stop the blight
in human thought; a mucky right of way
presenting its birdlife unnaturally.
But why trust, when trusting means deny the long
divined, the million booked, the clear
extinction that possesses every cell
of language, and every creature? Why do I,
a transcriber of trees, trust this path? Because
the curlew's verdict is so strange, I trust.

Anois Teacht an Earraigh

after Anthony Raftery

Now, with the advent of Spring,
and with brightness again marshalling my hours,
as I cross the threshold of Saint Brigid's Day,
the very centre of Mayo calls me to herself.
She begs me to take my seat in the heart of the county.
I'll go through Kiltimagh, my green
        and full-sailed heart parading.
Let the dying Winter glimpse me entering
        St Brigid's fold near Cill Aodáin,
now that Spring is near.
A creature of joyful flight and anticipation,
dreaming of the lakes, dreaming of berries
and all the innumerable wild fruit,
        unutterably sweet, in those parts;
within me, the teeming jewels of the names of the townlands.
I'll give nights freely to Claremorris, Ballinamore, and Milebush,
plumbing the wells of experience,
        until I become a dream that calls out:
'Speak to me, voice of Lough Carra, of things between
the parish lines; romantic fields north of yourself.'
And when the moment comes, mortality will
have no claim on my life; the light of kinship will see to that;
revealing the arc of St Brigid, and my people, in a moving circle,
great in their laughter, sure and wild in their dancing.

The May Baby

for Cecilia

translated from a version of a traditional Irish song
collected in County Monaghan by Henry Morris

Summer gold, akin to a flower's brightness;
this we carry with us,
in praise and celebration.

Girl of May, bounteous one, Summer's girl –
We bear you with us too, up hills, into valleys,
in praise and celebration.

A female team, clad in new effulgence,
we are touring now with the bough of Summer,
in praise and celebration.

The lark's performance extends the sky's blue,
tree blossom and insect life are one in broad passion,
and we bear the May girl, the Summer's self,
in praise and celebration.

We sing now to enumerate the hare's home
on the promontory, the grey heron high
in the branches, new grass thatched
by new honey beneath a loudness of doves.

Through these May things
we bear the Summer's garland,
and our May girl in the garland's heart;
arm in arm, in praise and celebration.

A Case of Cormorant Envy

Their crucifixion poses,
and their ignorance of fear,
and their free euphoric snorkelling
twelve months of the year.

Letter to a Harbour Seal

Further out the sea is energetically darkened.
There is the promise of a rotten afternoon.
Till then, under a blue sky, tall gusts deny
the tide and drive infernal milk across
the rocks. The forecast might be wrong, but all
the same I'll twist my words: 'We are promised
rotten weather, you and I.' On writing this I see
that coastal water has consumed the anchor
of my thinking. Clarity encircles, grips, combusts,
and now the changing sea instructs us: 'Look
at these two lives.' You, with your bronze moustache,
your scarred articulate shoulders, your glossy
air of clannish peace and long-journeying wonder.
And I, for love, almost identical.

An Archer

On a patch of recently dug up yard
that gets only a token of morning light
a vole appears. He has come in confusion
and sickness from his subterranean bed.
And now here he is, staggering along
and falling over, getting up quickly, then
kneeling. And then dramatically lying down
again. But only to convulsively rise,
his pink fists held out for balance, his black
eyes lit unequally by jets of pain.
Somehow he's not quite a miserable sight,
this sharply waistcoated man on shattered
stilts, this burdened boy unable to stop
grinning and unable to fear, this grey sprite
too stunned to see his human audience
or to resist being shipped in a giant's
hand and granted a night in a shoe box,
indoors, in a kitchen where after much
debate he is sounded out and baptized
with delicately prepared fruit morsels.
All who meet him are prey to sudden love.
All speak with love his little person's name.
And then, as if in return, he goes to work.
There is a kind of knowledge and a kind
of tide in the way his presence through the night
brings sequences of gifts: deep-rooted calm,
dream upon dream of the invisible yard,
a queer tonnage of rodent compassion,
with endless pictures of the insect realm.

By morning, the house is full of these wild
deposits, their imprints obvious in
our voices, in our eyes, and in our every
gesture at the cautiously conducted
burial given to the vole, the focal
point of which is a sunlit cot built from
dandelion stems and leaves. Deny it
as we might, pitch as we might cold reason
onto that exposed supply of wonder,
a story keeps its grip. How long had he
been ours? Not long at all. Had he a mission?
It made no sense to say he knew his powers;
and yet the slipstream of his death is full.
The whole thing, though ridiculous, rings true.
A messenger came with a clutch of arrows
and a flickering but peerless aim,
and he destroyed, one by one, in summer's name,
the things that want destruction in the mind.

In Loving Memory

Somewhere on this hill, which the locals
        refer to as the Sleeping Man,
there is a woodpecker. Not long ago,
        this same bird was not a bird at all,
but a human being. A teacher, in fact,
        a teacher of children in the town.

Something in his extended family turned sour.
        Jealousy, or the wrong word said,
or a moment of madness. Or perhaps
        a combination of all three. With these locals,
you could never guess. They're a petty
        and a strife-loving crowd. A crucifixion

is their *terra firma*. Give me, any day,
        the worst of bloodshed over
the worst of relatives. Anyway, something went wrong,
        and someone in the family
got their hands on the power to damn
        this poor man in this way, damn him

to a life of being a woodpecker,
        up here among the dire company
of all these State-planted spruces.
        It's hard to say which is worse, the life
of the habitat or the life of the inhabitants.
        But this, anyway, is the right place.

Any moment now we'll hear him.
        He tends to just start up out of the blue,
granting you the winged gift of imagining
        that he has been processing
your movements and your words,
        a gift that I find, at times, a great comfort.

We'll wait here at this spot a little longer.
        Patience, unfortunately,
is indispensable. The Sleeping Man
        and his mixed army of choristers,
I've found, are no respecters of time.
        And woodpeckers, you might say,

are the bird that is most alienated from the Irish clock.
        I was standing
right here, at this very spot,
        when I heard him last week. We'll give
it another ten minutes or so, and then,
        if nothing's doing, we'll hike

along the loop to the north ridge.
        The sea can be shockingly vivid
from the north side of the Sleeping Man.
        You will not be disappointed.
The forecast was for rain,
        and this morning we got all of this sun;

that's a reason to expect more good things.
He makes a truly wonderful sound,
greater than any woodpecker you'll ever hear.
He has his basic call, curt and clever
and lovely, and then he has the acoustic work
that he performs on the trees,

which is superbly loud. Too loud, you might say,
despite the fact that you are,
inevitably, transported. He's an engine,
an angel, a certifiable enchanter.
And yet, of course, it's hard not to think
of the curse that was put on him.

Is the sound he makes with a tree bole a great sound
(a sound that changes the valley)
because of the fact that inside the pressure
of his exile he manages to surrender
his full self to the fundamental music
of woodpecker existence?

Or is his former life forgotten?
Is he possibly a woodpecker who was once
a teacher of children in name only?
Is he a bird now like any other, with no dreams
and no story outside the traditional drill of his instincts?
There he goes!

How about that! How about that! Right on cue!
    Tell me now, to your mind, judging
by this evidence, would you say that
    he is at peace on the Sleeping Man,
that there is love in his drumming,
    and that he is not in hell? You see, I can't be sure.

My ears are biased. I'm too close to the family.
    I see his wife, awfully early, out walking.
What happens is this: I get so far in my listening
    and then I crash down among the giant
pine cones and the muck. Like a fool
    I keep coming back to the thought that he had
his whole life ahead of him. Tell me now,
    to your ears, has he mastered the curse?

BUAINE NA GAOITHE

A Waiting Tree

When I stop singing I hear a demon's voice.
He may have hiked along an inner path
until he found a clearing in my brain.
Other nights, by the lamp of my breathing,
he'll create inside my lungs a demon door.
He is a questioner: 'Will you not employ

your lost love? Will you not release that store
of golden grief for the sake of the song?'
Against these sharp requests, I've long maintained
were I to confess through indelible
imagery my incurable longing
my voice and I would be divorced at once.

'You pretend that you must not,' he barked one night,
retreating to the stairwell of my spine.
'Well, then, bold singer, despite your glory
it's no soul's evidence you give the world,
and it's not the world's sore need of melody
that you are ministering, claim what you will.'

For years, it's been no more troubling than this –
a heartful of hallucinated words,
an attack of cosmical soliloquy.
As such, I have felt indulged; until tonight.
I had sung to my limits again, bartered
my reason for the bell of existence,

plunged through the wonder of the choral tide,
becoming again the lark of innocence,
and, momentarily, the lark of death.
The last chords declined and my voice fell slow,
as ash through an ash-world of long applause.
But then, a rush of black analysis.

'A soul's hand brought internally to rest
on the emerald absence of your love –
this alone is singing, and this alone
the way to serve the being of the song.'
Enemy silence then, and then a curse.
'No,' I countered. 'Yes, yes,' the demon said,

calmer yet more repugnant than before,
which sent me first to fear, but then to rage,
so that I assumed a demon role myself
and battled that voice ecstatically, until
my open throat released a startled bird
for which my lost love was a waiting tree.

In Gortnagran

In Gortnagran, between two oaks,
a door was sometimes seen.
Some witnessed it opening,
some sensed an unlocked green.

Some, uneasy in their awe,
said the word door was wrong,
though door alone was image-kin
to this phenomenon.

I, among the madder ones,
knew that Gortnagran's role
in local-rooted, lunar things
encompassed herds of souls.

And, in particular, mother herds
(mothers centuries gone)
returned to perform cryptic plays
in Summer's female tongue.

There was a deal of waiting,
at times a deal of spoof,
but more than once the empty night
filled up with endless proof.

Those twin trees were embracing.
We watched them blend their glow;
before two dozen bridal ghosts
stepped through and staged a show.

Hopkins in the Basement of Saint Catherine's Bakery

From Catherine's heart I have borrowed sanity.
This morning, the dawn a hemorrhage of trust,
I ate a husk of bread and instantly
teams of devils were exiting my brain.
I heard a bitter ruckus on the stairs,
and then a sorry tumult in the lane.
And later, my mind eccentrically calm,
I heard them racing north and south at once.
Even now, with my madness restored,
I know they met death when they met the sea.
Tonight, Catherine, through the cloud of your mouth,
draw from the earth the element of pain.
Then once more make of one who adores you
a song-maker secure in caves of wheat.

A Merlin in the Sheeffrys

There is a feeling that is equal to the land,
a sense of self that is the journey's length.
It changes, bright to dark, and back again,
in moments such as when a hill decides
to vanish, prompting the sea to appear,
sun-thatched, sun-pregnant, sun-remonstrating,
before another bog-dividing mile
leads down to a stretch where abundant rock,
as if by words, or acts, elicits calm.
And then, in a mood of three mountains, you drive on,
the land's equal by free and strange degrees,
one for whom a merlin sighting proves a way
to push the day to absolute kinship.
The merlin declares: 'I have brought you here.'
To which madness the Sheeffry winds reply:
'Talk to the dead as you would to the living.
Address the living as if they were the dead.'

Her Crossings

There are mornings when,
simply by singing,

she sends herself
into the blackbird's world.

Off she goes,
the early sun, together with

her choice of song
and the body

of her willingness
forming a kind

of vessel;
within which, through her voice,

she perceives
a blackbird stationed

on the prow of life.
Aboard this marvel,

the way the blackbird's
rain-dressed manners

admit eternity
is a matter of love.

And in her crossings
this impact is key.

For she must fix the dawn
when human claws

have wrecked the solar gate,
and sing to resist

when songlessness
is king.

ACKNOWLEDGEMENTS

Thanks are due to the editors of the following publications where many of the poems in *The Meek* first appeared: *Poetry Ireland Review*; *Fortnight*; *Poetry*; *Winter Papers*; *New Hibernia Review*; *Manchester Review*; *Copper Nickel*; *Irish Times*; *Ogham Stone*; *Packingtown Review*; *Circle and Square: Platform One and Guests*, edited by Eileen Casey; *Windfall: Irish Nature Poems to Inspire and Connect*, edited by Jane Clarke; *Reading the Future: New Writing from Ireland Celebrating 250 Years of Hodges Figgis*, edited by Alan Hayes; *Town Stitched by River: Irish Writers at the International Writing Program*, edited by Christoper Merrill and Alan Hayes; *Reflection* (Irish Hospice Foundation); *Of Claws and Hooves and Meadows: 12 Poems for One Welfare* (Poetry Ireland).

Thanks are also extended to the Jackie Clarke Collection in Ballina; Mayo Arts Service; the Aidan Heavey Library in Athlone; Westmeath Arts Office; the School of English, Irish and Communication and the Creative Writing programme at the University of Limerick; the International Writing Program at the University of Iowa; the School of Medicine at Trinity College Dublin; An Tairseach Organic Farm and Ecology Centre, Wicklow; and to Alan Hayes, Paul Glavey, Lindsay McClelland, Deirdre Serjeantson, Richard Serjeantson, Jason Kelly, Darragh Golden, Francesca Nobili, Niamh Connolly, David Malee, Almar Ennis, Dermot Ennis, James Conry, Geraldine Parsons, Frank Shovlin, John Kenny, Keith Duggan, Enda Leaney, Patrick O'Sullivan, Michael Griffin, Benny Duggan, John Heneghan, Celine Broughal, Beatrice Heneghan, Bernard O'Donoghue, Bryan Patten, Caoimhe Ní Mhaolagáin, Claire Rumpsa, Sarah Burnes, Eilis O'Connell, Peter Barnfather, and the Dyar, Lavan, Scahill, and Lybeck families.

Fulsome and particular thanks to Alex Muller and Jefferson Holdridge at Wake Forest University Press for their creativity, professionalism, and care in bringing this book to fruition. And also to Anna Gramling, Abby McCabe, Carson Smith, and Alex Silverio, each of whom contributed to the finalising of *The Meek* during internships with the publisher.

'A Launch Night for Cogitosus' was commissioned by Kildare Library Service. Coinciding with the Brigid 1500 celebrations in 2024, Kildare Library Service commissioned and published a limited edition broadside version of the poem, with accompanying artwork by Stephen Pulbrook.

'Like a Soul' was written for *Mícheál Ó Súilleabháin: A Life in Music*, edited by Helen Phelan (UCC Press).

'In the Library' was commissioned by the Glucksman Library at the University of Limerick, and first published in the *Irish Times*, as part of a double sonnet written in collaboration with the poet Mary O'Malley.

The poems 'A Waiting Tree', 'In Gortnagran', 'Hopkins in the Basement of Saint Catherine's Bakery', 'A Merlin in the Sheeffrys', and 'Her Crossings' are from a song cycle titled *Buaine na Gaoithe*, which was written in collaboration with the composer Ryan Molloy and funded by an Arts Council Commission Award received by the Italian soprano Francesca Placanica. Liz Pearse (soprano), Chelsea Czuchra (flute), and Lindsay Buffington (harp), as Damselfly Trio, were the performers in a *Buaine na Gaoithe* Irish national tour in 2018.